AF431874

PIMPIN' TO PREACHIN'

Transforming From The Kingdom of Darkness to the Kingdom of Light

Charles Sims Jr.

SheEO PUBLISHING COMPANY

 Pimpin' to Preachin'

"Transforming the Kingdom of Darkness…to the Kingdom of Light"

By,

Charles Sims

Thank You

GOD

Prophet Jacqueline Sims

Dr. Winnie Hamilton

SonRise Global Ministries, Inc.

Apostle John H. Bibbens

Zion Church of Fredericksburg/
Lottsburg

Mildred Du'Mas

Charita Mariner

Ebony Sims

Tiffany Warner

Charles E. Sims, III

Charles L. Mayes

Kenny Saunders

Tonya Saunders

Linda Wollensen

Donnie Mason

Starr Mason

Angela Thomas

My Publisher,
Ari Squires

CONTENTS

FOREWORD

We have been together for almost half a century. I have known Charles since we were twelve years old. We went to Elementary School and Jr. High School together. At fourteen years old, we considered ourselves as "going together." We have been together for two thirds of our life.

During my High School years, I had to attend Jane Addams an all-girls school, which I hated, because it separated Charles and me. During that time, he began to have other girlfriends. Through it all, we found our way back together. A year after I graduated from High School, we were engaged to be married on Christmas Eve. On August 5, 1972, we tied the knot. We had a very large wedding, with family and friends. It was standing room only. Some haters said, "It will only last a year," but they were wrong. I have always wanted to have a family, husband, be a wife and raise children. This is why I fought for our marriage.

We have created a life and legacy with our three daughters and my stepson, with eleven grandchildren, and three great-grandchildren.

We have gone through love, heartache, joy and sorrow, and he has always protected me in my darkest hours…like there was no tomorrow. I pray for him. I cover him. I love him unconditionally. We vowed, "Until death do us part."

Prophet Jacqueline Sims, RN, Chaplain

To the man who taught me that "now FAITH is the substance of things hoped for, the evidence of things not seen" (Hebrews 11:1 KJV). Also, that if I had "FAITH as a grain of mustard seed" (Matthew 17:20 KJV) I could move mountains. My father has taught me to be a strong and mighty woman of God, who gives nothing than her best and accepts nothing less from anyone else. He has taught me to trust God in all that I do, so that I could fulfill my purpose.

To the man that refused to raise his family in the projects of Cleveland, because he believed there was something better and we deserved to be a part of it. You taught me what a father and husband should be. Daddy, you have taken my husband from being a broken man, to a man who is continuing to breakthrough. You have taught him how to be a husband, father, and mighty man of God. For this, I thank you and I love you.

Last, but not least. I am proud of the father and man you have been in our lives. I am glad that you have finally fulfilled your dream and your purpose of winning souls for the Kingdom of God by sharing your story of faith, perseverance, hope, and most of all, the Awesomeness of God!

Eternally Grateful & Blessed,

Tiffany Warner-Sims (Oldest Daughter)

The strangest thing is looking at someone as if you are looking in a mirror from the future…. My father and I share more than DNA; we share good looks, charm and an "over-standing" of the "female persuasion", we share an indigenous desire to know the truth.

I have memories of my father cutting my hair in the bathroom as I sat still, mesmerized by his aura and the aroma of Turbo cologne. All I could think was, "one day, I'll be as big and strong as he is." Every chance I got to spend time with him, I would watch him like a hawk. Studying his bow-legged walk, his mannerisms, and most importantly, how he dealt with his ol' lady, "Mrs. Jackie." Mrs. Jackie was fine, and I could see why she caught his eye. It takes a special lady to get men like us to settle down and have three beautiful babies!

Ha Ha Lol, yeah over the years, me and father have grown to love and appreciate the time we get to converse with one another. The content of our conversation would freeze a fly's wings as it sat on a wall tryna soak up game being swapped. Many hours have been logged with us trying to figure out what is life really about. We've discussed and sometimes debated religion, spirituality, politics, relationships and pimpin', to name a few.

I'll never forget the time my father cried when I told him I wasn't mad at him for having another family. "At 19 or 20, I know how I was with women. I had several girls I would party with. I get it now that I'm grown. Y'all were young and having fun. The 70s didn't require the use of condoms like the 80s or 90s!" (*Lucky me*)

You see, there really isn't much difference between me and my father. I'm a lil bit younger, a lil bit faster, and a lot more handsome but overall...

"He is I, and I am him, slim with the tilted brim!"

Love you Pop

Charles Laray (Oldest Son)

The Word of God says in Ephesians 6:1-3, "*Children obey your parents in the Lord for this is right. Honor your father and mother which is the first commandment with promise. That it may* *be well with you and you may live long on the earth." **I've always tried to please my parents in everything that I do.***

My Father is a Blessing of a Man that I was named after, Charita. I am the middle child that doesn't have the middle child syndrome. He makes me laugh until my ribs are hurting, snot running out of my nose and I'm rolling on the floor. His Shenanigans is just way too much and I wouldn't trade him for the World. Surprisingly, he wasn't always this funny though until his older years (50+). He was always so focused on being a hard-nosed, religious minded Pastor and not a dad that told his children he loved them—or even hugged them. My Dad's reason for not being affectionate was the thought of girls being molested by their fathers. He never wanted that to be said of him. He wanted to stay with his girls and not raise us in the projects. Even though he was a preacher who had three daughters with babies out of wedlock, he stuck in to help raise his Grandsons. He never had an example of what a father or husband was supposed to be like. He just knew that he would always be there to provide for us. See, we learned later that maybe because of his past relationship with his father; it had direct impact on his affection towards his children. He had to learn by trial and error.

Let me be clear, my daddy loves us to no end and made sure we had whatever we needed as far as we knew it. I clearly remember a time that was really fun for us and that was when we met our Stepbrother. He was 7 years old with a white karate suit and we were so amazed at him. I was just happy to have a brother since all I had was 2 sisters that I was forced to share clothes that I purchased, and worked hard for everyday. My father loves my Brother, Charles, who looks just like him. Consequently, in that day and time or even neighborhood, he really was concerned with protecting his girls and making sure we didn't end up dating our brother and didn't know it. Side Note: My Brother is Fine and we ended up in the same school, so a relationship, could've happened if we didn't know better.

My dad was not a real affectionate dad and when we said, "We love you daddy!", he would say, "Y'all Alright" verses "I Love

You All". This stuck with us for years and we mess with him about it to this day. Now, we can't keep him out of our face with hugs and much Love!! Smiling, kissing us, hugging everyday and trying to get us to eat food or drink after him???? Imagine that. Now, we laugh about having too MUCH LOVE and affection from him! He's #Team2Much, but we wouldn't trade this Anointed Man of God, Friend, Great Male Role Model, Papa, Strong Black Man and Father, for nothing in this world!

I Love you Daddy!

Charita R. Mariner (Middle Daughter)

As for me and my house we will serve the Lord (Joshua 24:15 KJV). This scripture is the Covenant my father made well before I came into this world. Glory be to God!! I'm overwhelmed with excitement for you. Finally, you are able to discover the greatness of Apostle Charles Sims. To sit at his feet countless times and listen to him preach life into my spirit, soul and body has been priceless. I remember thinking as a believer, he is so rare and his message is out of this realm. As his daughter, I thought how blessed I was to be able to listen to him. Whenever he spoke, he would begin to glow right in front of me. Whether it be in the kitchen or in the pulpit; I could see the power of God shower him like sun rays. Oh, what a good time we would have in the Lord! As you reap your harvest, prepare to grow in your understanding of the Lord and his ways. Find out how life was meant to be lived with Jesus and learn the mysteries behind the scriptures that only God can reveal. I'm so grateful to have this wonderful man be my spiritual leader, counselor and most of all, my father. I pray that God blesses all who read this book and may God continue to bless you dad on this amazing journey. Love you much.... Babygirl.

Ebony Sims (Youngest Daughter)

PREFACE

Joseph was the eleventh and youngest son of Jacob. He was his father's favorite and was treated that way. Jacob even made Joseph a special robe of many colors, which caused simmering resentment among his brothers. Joseph would help his brothers care for the family's sheep and goats. Jacob instructed Joseph to report back any of his siblings' misdeeds, which caused even more bitterness.

When he was seventeen, Joseph had two dreams that indicated one day he would be a ruler. His brothers became openly hostile at such an idea and devised a plan to kill him. The brothers did this out of pride and jealousy, not understanding the plan God had for Joseph. This part of Joseph's life I can relate to. Sometimes you are misunderstood because of the choices you make.

Joseph was spared death at the urging of his brother, Reuben. Instead, they threw him into a pit to teach him a lesson. But when they happened to see a caravan passing by, they took the opportunity to sell Joseph into slavery. They lied and told their father he was killed by an animal, and used his blood-soaked robe as proof.

For years, Joseph was a slave in Egypt. His master was Potiphar, captain of Pharaoh's guard. Accepting his fate and trusting in God, Joseph became Potiphar's personal servant and later ran his household. After Joseph rejected the romantic advances of Potiphar's wife, she lied and claimed he had tried to rape her. Her false accusations landed Joseph in prison.

Even though God had given him a vision of future greatness, Joseph had to go through this dark time in his life. You may ask why would God allow this to happen to him? I believe that God was seasoning him for a time where he would not be denied. Everyone that hurt him would eventually need him, see greatness in him, and know that he was truly chosen by God.

Joseph's gift for interpreting dreams won his freedom. The pharaoh was troubled by dreams of lean cows eating fat cows. Joseph explained it as foretold seven years of abundance followed by seven years of famine and told the pharaoh to start stockpiling grain and other food.

Joseph was released from prison and appointed the pharaoh's vizier, or right-hand man. Now a respected advisor to the pharaoh, Joseph married and had two children.

When the famine struck, people from all across the land came to Egypt, which had ample food—thanks to Joseph. Among those seeking help were his brothers, who didn't recognize him, but Joseph recognized *them.* Joseph could have left them to starve or had them imprisoned. Instead, Joseph became the man that God created, forgave his brothers, and saved his family.

I'm sharing this story because I have been in the darkness. I've been wronged by friends, by people who said they would always be there. I have done wrong to others as well. I have been a womanizer, cheater, liar, a pimp, and a drug addict. I never thought that with everything I had done in my life that God could use me and yet, you will see through my testimony that God was able to still use the gift deep inside of me.

In this book, you will see my life-changing transitions: youth, marriage, pimping, military, acceptance of Jesus Christ, and the Apostle of God.

I'm not perfect. I am a work in progress, and God has brought me a mighty long way. I have had to learn to forgive those who hurt me. I had to take that journey and sit down and be honest about who I was and what I was doing with what I thought was my life. I now know that without God I could never live what I call *my life*.

"For without Me you can do nothing" (John 15:5 AKJV).

That is what I want for you in your life. I want you to be able to discover the true gift that God has placed inside of you; the *you* God sees. That is the one that can help lead you out of the darkness.

I thank God for a great wife and the people who were brought in my path as part of my journey for the seasons, lessons, and blessings. I also thank Him for His mercy and grace that is unconditional and everlasting.

I pray the words on these pages and my testimony of God's grace will show you that even when you have been left for dead, God will resurrect you if you hold onto your faith. I want you to know that there is a light up ahead. You may not feel it or know it for sure, but His plan will work out. I know simply because I am a living testimony.

Before I sat down to write my story, I asked myself a couple of questions, and I would like to share them with you.

Did you know that God has created you with a seed of potential, and if you use it you will discover the real person who lives inside of you?

I realized that this is what happened to me, and you will see why I say that as you read on.

If you understand His important message—you have a seed of potential—you will be able to see yourself as He sees you: whole, mighty, worthy, and full of purpose.

How do we connect with the God that lives deep inside of us?

If you can see yourself through God's eyes, then and only then can you find out who you really are and what your purpose is while you're here on Earth; a true child of the highest God.

God tells us in His word that we were made in His image; we are in His likeness. Nonetheless, we have not tried to find out what that true image of God is that lives in us. It's simple: He has laid out the plan in His word. He tells us that we are "wonderfully and fearfully made" (Ps. 139:14 KJV).

We are constantly looking outside of ourselves for the answer in things such as money, education, famous people, vacations, and the lifestyles we see on television and in the neighborhood.

We have always been more prone to try to find out who we want to be instead of allowing God to really show us who we are supposed to be. Since God's purpose is greater than our own, He wanted me to live in His purpose instead of my own. Because of my stubbornness, God had to come into my life and allow some things to happen to me in order to get my attention. Unfortunately, when you don't listen to God, pain and sorrow will be your outcome.

I don't want you to go through what I experienced. I want you to know that there are great things promised to you. Now I can see that I don't have to live in poverty, shame, and defeat.

I understand completely because I didn't always know who I was. So during my journey, I decided a few of things had to take place for me to reach God's full potential for me.

I decided that I wanted my life to have value, to have meaning and to help people. I want others to read what I'm writing and to really digest what I'm saying.

I can hear it now…

I can relate to that.

I need to do that.

I need to do exactly what he did.

I need to follow his guidance.

That's the direction that I need to go because I never knew what direction I needed to take before.

A lot of people need direction in life and a lot of people need answers that we just don't have. I believe God is using my life and my story to help others. You may not feel valuable or worthy and certainly not worthy of His grace, but if He can show me who I was—a little black boy born into poverty in the fifties to a young mother with no father figure—I know He can do it for you too. I am sure of it!

God has something greater in store for me, something better. I am valuable to Him, and He has designed me with greatness. It's better than what I saw for myself, yet I wasn't always aware. Nonetheless, I did know there had to be something else to my life other than just struggles and having so many unanswered questions.

No matter what anybody says, we all question God to some extent. I often wondered things like: *Why do I exist? What am I here for? What is my destiny?* I have spoken to so many people over the years who have experienced the same struggle, who have asked themselves the very same questions. Some people even commit suicide because they don't know who they really are and never fully understand why they exist. They cannot see the true unconditional seed of divine value that is placed inside of them.

I now know who I am according to I Thess. 5:23[1]; I am a spirit with a soul and live in a body—in that order.

I pray that my vision for this book will lead you down the path of finding your self-worth, and understanding that God's grace is truly sufficient. The bible says, "Your word is a lamp unto my feet and light unto my path" (Ps. 119: 105 KJV).

So sometimes you need the path lit to help guide you, to better see where you're trying to go. You need to see the rocks—the obstacles and challenges—so you can avoid them. God's light will help you see down that dark, winding road. Believe me;

---

1 *And the very God of peace sanctify you wholly; and I pray God your whole spirit and soul and body be preserved blameless unto the coming of our Lord Jesus Christ.*

there are many winding roads that will take you places you never intended to go. God brings clarity to your situation.

I think the reason we all move in darkness and end up someplace that could have been avoided, is because we are relying on our own understanding (Prov. 3:5 NIV), and that's our biggest mistake. It gets us in trouble.

My hope is to turn the light on in dark places. To shine a light in the dark pathways of life, so you can see clearly down the path of truth. To help you avoid many of the hardships and struggles I've experienced. To see that God has much more in store for you and for your life. No matter what you've planned for yourself, it will never be able to compare to what He has in store for you.

1

THE BOY

Born and raised in the ghetto just trying to survive without a father who walked out my life.

~ Charles Sims

I know the reason why my life was so dark as a child. God planned for my life to serve others and help them understand their purpose.

Growing up was a struggle. The oldest boy of eight siblings, I was raised by my single mom. My father left when I was two, so I never knew what it was like to have a dad in my life. He was never there for me and a boy needs his father, you know? There's a void, and it just feels like an empty space that can never be filled. You're susceptible to being wounded or hurt. So I know that's why I did the things I did. I didn't understand the sinful life. I had no knowledge where a life totally influenced by evil or the evil one (Satan) could take you.

I know my mother did the best she could, but there are some things that only a man can teach his son. I didn't have that iron-sharpens-iron experience. If you didn't have your father in your life like me, you understand that. I'm not sure if I was angry at him for not being there, or just hurt. But I never had him in my life, and I imagine that's what I needed. I had to do a lot of things on my own. I had to grow up fast.

Since I was the oldest son, my mother depended on me to take on responsibilities I wasn't ready for like helping take care of my siblings. She would always say: *You're the man,* and did the best to make me think that I was the man, spiritually and naturally. But I was still just a boy who desperately needed a father. When you're forced to grow up fast, you never get the opportunity to live out your boyhood. You miss out on some things you really need.

That's what happened to me. Back in the day, we learned what it meant to be a man from watching our older male relatives, neighbors, and family friends. Instead of having a father as a role model, I looked up to my mom's only brother. For as long as I can remember, he was an inspiration to me, in an interesting kind of way.

MY EXAMPLES WERE ALL I HAD

My good ole Uncle Fred was my inspiration and I paid attention to everything he did and said. I used to watch him like a hawk: the way he walked, talked, and laughed. I used to look at how cool he was and how women—and he had a lot of women— followed his every command.

I used to admire the way he dealt with people. He commanded respect from everyone, and in my eyes he could do no wrong. At the time, I wanted to be just like him. As you could imagine, not everyone in my family was happy with me wanting to be like my uncle.

Later in my adult life, my mother would always say, "He was the devil in your life."

Considering the destructive path that it led me down and the choices and decisions I considered for my life, she had her reasons for saying that. If I had really listened to my mother as a young boy, if I had paid closer attention, things would have turned out differently.

I was very impressionable, so she was constantly telling my uncle, "Leave that boy alone."

My mother was just trying to protect me because she knew things that I didn't. She instinctively knew what my uncle was all about and what he stood for. But because I was just a boy, I could not grasp it. I was young and didn't really understand how the world worked or fully comprehend his lifestyle. I only saw his material things in life.

He had the drugs, the women, and the money in his pockets. He made everything look so easy, especially the way he acquired all those things. I never could quite understand what exactly he did. I just knew he had it.

To be honest, I didn't know what drove him to all of that. I can only assume that he wanted the same things all males want: to feel like a man, to have nice things, to have the respect of other guys in the neighborhood, to have the best women, and a flamboyant lifestyle. That was just how life used to be in the ghetto.

Looking back now, I know that listening to my mother; that would have been the best thing that could have ever happened to me. Her words would have stopped me from going down a path of destruction. Maybe it was how I grew up, where I grew up, or the times I grew up in. Whatever it was it was, my choices and decisions led me down my path.

THE GOOD OL' DAYS

I grew up in Cleveland, Ohio, in the 1960s. Our country was going through many changes at that time. It was the era of the Civil Rights Movement, interracial love coming out of the racial closet, and rhythm and blues music going mainstream. Tensions were high around the country between whites and black Americans.

As you could imagine, it was an interesting time for me. I was born in 1953 and the world looks very different today than it was in the mid-twentieth century. Back in the day, it was more of a deep, dark struggle amongst those in the black neighborhoods. Life in the 50s and 60s was when you'd stand in line for government-provided cheese, peanut butter, and powdered milk. Those were times when your mom would send you next door or down the street to ask a neighbor lady for a bowl of flour or sugar and you would return it later. Those were times when you could get credit from the neighborhood store and your parents would pay the owner on their payday.

That was the era I grew up in. It wasn't easy, but it wasn't all bad either. So even though it was hard growing up back then, what I loved about it most was the neighborhood. Everybody knew everybody. It was really cool how all of the families were connected and united back then. Nothing would go down in the neighborhood without everybody knowing about it. It truly was something special how we really were our brothers' keeper.

I have to say I liked those times better because our young people had more discipline. Parents were a little stricter than parents are today. You would get your clothes ready for church on Saturday night, and if you didn't go to church on Sunday, you could forget going to the movies or anyplace else. With all the laws and new ideas on raising children today, it makes it harder to discipline. You cannot raise a man without discipline, or he will go astray and go down the wrong path. I see that problem with a lot of our boys and young men today. Earthly things that have no real spiritual value are leading them astray.

As I was coming up in life, I lived in the ghettos of Cleveland having to share with my seven brothers and sisters. I really loved my siblings, but you don't have the same opportunities as children with fewer siblings. I was sad when they had things I didn't because we had more people in our household and less money. Things were passed down in my house from one sibling to the other over and over again.

Some people may be able to relate to what I'm saying, especially those who didn't have enough to share, but still had to. You're forced to live with a smile, even when you're hurting. You learn to put others before you, even when you don't want to. It hurt me sometimes as a young boy.

My mother did the best that she could to stretch money; even so, there was only so much she could do raising us on a measly income. But my mother was the kind of woman who would do what was necessary to provide for her children no matter what. My siblings and I didn't really approve of everything my mother did in front of us, but there wasn't much we could do about it. We knew why she was doing the things she did. We learned early on to keep our mouths shut and to respect our elders, especially our mother. It really affected me as a young boy, and I know it affected my siblings as well.

My mother was dating, so we never had one constant man that we could look at as a father figure. My mom had two regular men who came in and out of our house. We figured out what she was doing by putting two and two together. We never paid much attention to it because we knew that she was doing it in order to keep our household moving forward. I believe different things contributed to me traveling down a dark path and seeing those different men was one of them. Even though it wasn't said, you start to think it's okay. I started to believe that was how things were supposed to be because no one told me differently, especially where I'm from.

My mom used to throw card parties and all my aunts would come over. My mom would also invite her girlfriends. I don't know what it is, but I always had a real interest in light-skinned women and was infatuated by them as a young boy. So when I was five or six, I'd hide under the table while they were all sitting around playing cards, so I could see their soft, smooth, light-skinned legs. And I'd caress them.

When I first started doing it, the women would say, "Get up from under there, boy!"

I would be under there smiling like a little kid with a lollipop at the candy store. Then it got to a point where when my mom told me to stop and get out from under the table, I just wouldn't pay her any attention. And someone would say, "Aww, leave him alone. That's just Charlie under there."

They wouldn't even jump anymore. They stopped caring, so being a mannish little boy was something that started early for me. Those kinds of things turned me on. I was harmless back then, but I really believe it started me down a path that wasn't in my best interest. Getting involved with women in that way early in my childhood probably opened doors for me to live a promiscuous life.

A BOY BEING A BOY

As I got older, I started paying attention to other things too. Like how we were poor. I could see the difference between my family and other families. I realized that we didn't have nice things or a nice home, which impacted me mentally and socially. I felt bad about myself because I was embarrassed by where we were living and how we were living.

While everyone else was coming to school with new clothes and nice stuff, we wore family hand-me-downs and cheap clothes from the Goodwill although our clothes were always clean. We lived in roach-infested—sometimes even rat-infested—homes. I hated that. I truly resented being poor because it made me feel helpless; there wasn't anything I could do. I had to watch my mother try to take care of all eight of us all by herself.

When you're a child, you don't always understand why you have to live in horrible conditions. I would just get angry at times and just want to fight for no reason at all. I was a young boy becoming a young man in difficult times, and we had nothing but love to hold us together.

I certainly felt the gravity of poverty; it weighed on me. If you were not at the table by 5:30 for supper, there was no food left for you. Everything would already be eaten up, because there were so many of us and so little food. We used to always ask our friends what time it was so we wouldn't be late. If I was, my mom would say, "I told you to be home."

I'd think, *Dag what am I going to do now? What am I going to eat?*

Back then, I frequently went to bed hungry. It was the worst feeling. And that emptiness in your stomach is enough to make you angry. Yet, there wasn't anything I could do but go to sleep. Looking back on it now, it's kind of funny realizing that having a poverty mindset was what blinded me and later my wife because it followed us growing up.

Realizing my mom needed help, I had to do something. I was slowly becoming a young teen, and I had to start bringing money into the house to help out. My mother loved that I was willing to do anything to help her. She was a hard-working woman, and I believe I got my work ethic from her. She really admired that quality about me.

I learned how to hustle because I could not bear to keep watching her struggle. As a matter of fact, my hustle was inspired by my mother. I would go around the neighborhood and hustle up all the pop bottles, because I could get two cents for them and five cents for some of the bigger pop bottles. I had a paper route, so I learned how to go out in the neighborhood and ask everybody for their payment. I would get up early in the morning, pick up my newspapers, then roll by the houses in my neighborhood, and throw all the papers accurately on the porches. It was the beginning of creating my own hustle.

All of the people in the neighborhood knew me, and I had a great reputation. I was a very friendly little boy, plus everybody knew and loved my family. Growing up in Cleveland I remember meeting a famous football player. If you knew this NFL player, you were *the man*. This player was legendary to children in the neighborhood, and I was his paperboy because he lived on the same street that we lived on.

I loved being his paperboy because at Christmas, he would always give me a football with his signature. I wish I had them to this day, but through all the moves in life, I wasn't able to keep track of possessions with sentimental value. We were not even thinking about the financial value because that's not how we thought in those days. Back then, children were just children. We did things for the love of it, even though it was a struggle, I learned a lot, and it helped make me the man I am today.

Growing up the way I did taught me responsibility. I always helped my mom, and when I gave my earnings to her, it would be right when she needed it. She would say, "Charlie, boy if you had not gave this money to me today, I don't know what we would've done."

I learned early in life to have multiple hustles. I also knew how to shine shoes. I would get anywhere from fifty cents to seventy-five cents for each pair. It might not sound like a lot of money, but it was all good back in the day because you were able to buy a lot with a dollar such as bologna, milk, and bread. Any type of income was helpful to my mother, no matter how small.

She really knew how to make a dollar stretch. Sometimes I hated it because I wanted to buy myself some candy and treats for doing my hard work, but she normally would take it all, and I would say okay. Every now and then, I would get a nickel or dime, but that didn't stop me from working to help my mom and family. I knew she needed it more than me. Plus, that's what boys do; we help take care of things. I knew my mother was grateful.

When I was a young boy, my mom took me to work with her. She worked at hotels in downtown Cleveland so we would take the bus to get there. I hated that she had to go to this job. I was scared because she would run across all sorts of different things while she worked. She used to find dead people who were murdered or who had overdosed on drugs.

There was a restaurant near her job that she would take me to. The owner of the restaurant was a big Italian guy who loved my mother and she said they were really good friends. She would tell him, "I'ma leave him here while I go to work and I'll come back and get 'em."

I really enjoyed being in his restaurant because I got a chance to feel like an only child for once. The restaurant owner would give me a big hamburger and a coke, sit me in a booth, and say, "Now you stay right there until your mother comes and gets you."

I would have a ball because it was hard for me to get that kind of a meal at home, but he was that kind of a guy, and he took care of me. Those were some good times. I still remember how good that big ol' hamburger used to taste. I ate fast because I was so hungry, trying to savor every bite. It was like I was in heaven. It may not sound like much, but growing up how I did, you learn to appreciate the small things in life more.

He used to call her by her first name, Mary. When she would get back from her hotel job, he would say, "Hey, Mary, he's back here."

My mother also took me with her because sometimes on the way home she'd stop at the store and buy groceries for the week, with the money she earned at the hotel. Back then, we had to carry the bags home because we didn't have a car; we were on foot. Every few blocks, we had to put our grocery bags down and rest. Then we'd pick them back up, walk about another block, and put them down again. We did this all the way home.

Sometimes, I would see some of my friends along the way and they would help us carry the bags home so we didn't have to keep stopping. That is one thing I loved; the neighborhood children adored my family so they didn't mind helping out. We played and fought hard on the playground, but they respected my mother and called her mom too. That made me feel good.

My mother had a lot of children around who weren't her own. There were eight of us so we had a lot of friends coming around. My brothers, sisters, and I filled the house with the neighborhood children. We were living in poverty, but they didn't care. I was embarrassed because they would see roaches running around, but our friends just wanted to be with us; as kids they didn't care about materialistic things—at least not back then.

There were times when we would hear rats running inside the walls and they were reproducing rapidly. My brother and I would get so tired of it, we would take chains and place them against the doorway, and we would meticulously patrol the house with our airsoft BB guns looking for rats. It seemed like anytime we killed one, three more would come out of the woodwork. We used to watch them jump from the floor, to the counter, to the trash can, and as soon as they jumped into the sink, we would accurately align our sights and try to kill as many as we could.

One time, my brother was using the bathroom and a rat jumped out of the toilet between his legs while he was doing his business. I remember it like it was yesterday. My brother frantically ran into the kitchen with his pants still down attempting to tell us what happened, but we were all laughing too hard. That was just one of the many ways we made light of our living situation.

I believe that part of my life instilled in me that it was important to keep a job and keep money in my pocket. Even as a young boy, I was a hard-worker. I wanted better for myself I learned that you had to have money if you wanted the best, and I wanted the best.

I had an Uncle, Larry who was almost the opposite of my other uncle. He would do a lot for me as a young boy like take me to the West Branch of the Chagrin River on Route 422. He taught me everything I needed to know about fishing, from putting the bait on the hook to casting. I would go fishing with Uncle Larry every chance that I got. He would pack a lunch and we would sit by the river listening to his radio or talk about fishing. He would tell me old stories about his life. I can still hear the radio playing.

What was really exciting was when we listened to baseball games on the radio. We would sit there by the murky waters for hours. I enjoyed that part of my younger years the most. It was a great escape to be out there on the water enjoying the breeze and all that nature had to offer. But I knew I had to go back to my everyday life, my reality. I don't think anyone would choose to be poor. Sometimes we don't always know how to get out of poverty so we end up just adapting to the lifestyle. I know now that being poor creates a poor mindset, but with God's grace, we can change our minds, change our situation, and change the way we think about things.

EVERY PERSON WHO COMES INTO YOUR LIFE IS THERE FOR A REASON AND A SEASON

Growing up as a kid, I was a short, little guy. I didn't really start growing until I was about fourteen or fifteen years old, and I know that affected how I saw myself. My self-esteem was already low from living in poverty and not having the basics like new or nice clothes. If you have never gone through experiences like that, it may be hard for you to truly grasp how that can have impact on you. I often felt bad about myself, until I met my father's sister.

I must have been around nine or ten years old when I met my father's sister, Aunt Rosetta. She was a godsend and played a huge role in me and my sister's lives. My mother had three children with my father—me and my sisters. My other five siblings had a different father. My father left when I was a toddler so we really didn't know my father's sister until years later.

Aunt Rosetta owned a dry cleaning business and she began teaching my second oldest sister and me different jobs there, like how to make hangers for the men's pants, how to fold them, and how to press the shirts and dresses. Aunt Rosetta also taught my sister how to run the counter so she wouldn't have to stop whatever work she was doing to go wait on people. Having us there helped her out quite a bit. It was also good for me and my sister too because we got a chance to learn something very valuable. We learned how to work together as a family, and that we could take care of one another. My sister enjoyed it so much and became very good at her job. My Aunt would give me and my sister money on the side for helping her out, which meant so much to me.

You know, back in the 1950s and '60s, ten or fifteen dollars was a lot of money. Sometimes if business was good and we were really helpful, she would give us up to twenty-five dollars! With our pockets full of money, I began to see myself differently…as better. I could finally see a little light in my life.

There was a local department store called Rosenblum. It was a very expensive store and Aunt Rosetta had a store card because that's where she shopped. Every blue moon, she would give my sister the card and tell her to take me with her downtown to Rosenblum's.

When we got there, we'd say to each other, "She must be crazy—*look at these prices!*"

We never, ever experienced wearing alpaca or mohair sweaters, which were popular back then. That was the first time I was able to have some nice, expensive clothes. Thanks to my Aunt, we started looking sharp when we went to school. We walked around looking and feeling much better about ourselves, and that helped my self-esteem.

I thank God she showed up when she did. She unquestionably helped us along the way with building up our esteem and how we felt about ourselves. Even if she didn't say it, Aunt Rosetta really trusted us and helped change our situation. We got accustomed to making money and having a steady income.

She had these Maxwell House coffee cans that she would keep all of her change in. Those cans were full of coins. She had it good. She kept all this change in the kitchen of her house, which was behind the business. So she would just walk to the back of the cleaners, step down the stairway into the kitchen, and dump her change.

Like a lot of our elders back then, my aunt didn't believe in putting her money in a bank. So she would always hide it under the carpet or in her mattress—she stashed it all around the house. After she passed away, the carpeting was removed and they found money. The money was so old that it was crumbled and fell apart. Obviously, she hid money in so many places that even she forgot where it all was.

My mom was happy because the money that Aunt Rosetta gave us helped put more food on our table. We struggled a little less, and my mother felt good knowing she had more than enough to feed us. We thanked God for Aunt Rosetta because nobody had to worry about when their next meal would be. I guess you could say that things had begun to look up after Aunt Rosetta came into our lives and we were living a little larger compared to how we lived previously. It was a great thing to experience after being poor for so long.

I was ecstatic and felt like things were about to change for this little, poor black boy born on the wrong side of town. You know how they say, *Christmas in July*? It was like that for us because she showed us another side to life. Aunt Rosetta helped me and my sister and gave us the opportunity to share the wealth of her life and catch our breath a little bit.

THE POWER OF INFLUENCE

My father started showing up at the cleaners to see his sister, but we didn't really know him. We had not seen our father since he left us. He would show up out of nowhere in this beautiful car. My father was a ladies' man too and even though he was an older guy, he was known for liking younger girls. When I saw the girls that he was with, I'd say to my aunt, "She could be *my* girlfriend."

"Yeah," she'd respond, "he likes 'em young."

My father's name was Charles too; I am a junior. When he came into the store, my aunt called him Chuck. One day my aunt said, "Hey Chuck do you know who this is? These yo children."

It was a shame because he didn't have a clue as to who we were or where we came from. So the first time we met him, he shook his head with assurance and said, "Na."

Then my aunt said, "Dat's the love child."

He said to me, "Come here, boy."

I remember this moment like it was yesterday. I walked over and looked him up and down a few times, checking out his appearance. I noticed every detail about him. He was a slick guy, gold in his mouth, hair done from a beautician, the whole nine yards. He was what we called a smooth cat, and I didn't expect my father to be that kind of guy. I had so many thoughts and questions running through my head. I didn't know if I was happy, angry, hurt, or sad. That's the thing; I don't think he realized how much it affected me by him not being there.

Auntie then leaned over to him and said, "Dat's your daughter."

So then, he called my sister over to him, and looked at her.

And that is how we got to know him: by coming by the cleaners helping out our Aunt Rosetta. He'd visit his sister regularly so we became very familiar with him. I used to wonder if that was all part of my aunt's plan to get our father involved in our lives. Even if that was the case, he never became a real part of our lives. He never took us anywhere or acted like a father figure. Every now and then, he would give us five or ten dollars. I guess that was his way of feeling like he was actually contributing in some way.

But it wasn't enough. That couldn't give me the father back that I longed for. I knew that he was our father, but he had to earn the title of being a father. He was just a regular person that we knew, someone almost like a friend. We imagined a real father to be loving, supportive, and active in our lives. He certainly didn't meet those standards.

As I mentioned my mother's brother, my Uncle Larry had a lot of influence on my life growing up. So did my Uncle Fred, who was what I thought a man should be—his lifestyle, the women, the cars, and everybody liking him. Whenever Uncle Fred was in the area, he'd come to my mom's house to check on her, give her money, and see us kids to make sure we were all alright.

He would come find me if I was at the playground or playing football on the street. Back in the day, everybody used to play in the streets, and we had so many games we played. We were always outside, watching cars coming down the street, and everyone would say, "Here comes your uncle."

Every time I saw him, he was in a nice car. And it was always a Cadillac or a 225 Buick Electric, also known as a *deuce and a quarter*. That played a big part in why everybody in my neighborhood looked up to him. They respected him, and every man desires to be respected. That made a huge impact on me. He had everything most men desire, or at least that's what I thought.

If my mother was sitting on the porch, she would look happy when my uncle pulled up—he always had two or three girls in the car. I would think to myself: *Now how is that possible?*

I'd run to the car to see the pretty ladies. They smelled good even though they were smoking cigarettes, drinking alcohol, and doing anything else. To me, it seemed they were having fun. That's why every time my uncle and I were together, my mother would see a gleam in my eyes. And why she told him to leave me alone because she saw how much I respected and admired my uncle and knew what he was up to.

He was her brother and she loved him, but she didn't want me getting tied up in his lifestyle. She wanted me to have a different life for myself. On the other hand, my uncle was constantly telling me, "You'll have it like this someday."

During my quiet moments, I'd hear him saying that to me in my head, and I started to believe it. I started to tell myself: *Yeah, I am going to be like that one day*. He stayed in my life as a constant reminder of that big man lifestyle.

Back then, the term "big man" meant to be a hotshot, shot caller, or a popular person of interest to the community. He *could* have steered me in the direction of being a basketball player, or something that could have made more of a positive impact in my life; but instead, he was training me to think like him, do things just like him, and be like him.

And he made a big impression on me at a young age. In my little mind, all I could think was: *Oh man, this is it! I have to be like him.* I know now as an adult that everything that glitters ain't gold; just because something looks good on the outside, it's not necessarily good for you—and it's not all that it appears to be.

But sometimes you have to learn those lessons for yourself. I learned a lot from going down that path, and now I want to help others understand that you don't have to choose the wrong path. You can make better decisions to prevent an outcome that could be detrimental to your future.

As you read this, let my life story influence you in the right way by showing you that there will be many glitter moments on your journey; but take heed that those same moments and decisions can take you down the wrong path. We all have the ability to influence, so we must be careful when we are speaking into others' lives.

BE CAREFUL. THERE'S AN ORDER.

The lesson here is knowing what you have to do. The bible says in 1 Corinthians 2:14 KJV, "But the natural man receives not the things of the Spirit of God: for they are foolishness unto him: neither can he know them, because they are spiritually discerned".

When you're being influenced, you have to be aware of what's influencing you and what part of you is leading the way. If you're under the influence of your body, well, of course, you're going to be body conscience or led by what you see with the physical eye—like I was with my uncle—and that will lead you to be controlled by your flesh.

The bible says: "For they that are after the flesh do mind the things of the flesh; but they that are after the Spirit the things of the Spirit." (Romans 8:5 KJV)

2

MY TEENAGE YEARS

I could not process why my mind was steering me in the direction of my Uncle Fred. In my eyes, it wasn't wrong to crave the lifestyle that he possessed. Even though I didn't quite understand what the *path of sin* was, I had some knowledge between right and wrong. But because I was blinded by my fleshly desires, I began to go down the path of corruption and destruction. I was growing up. I was becoming a teenager.

I spent a lot of time at the playground as a teenager. One day, a pretty, young light-skinned girl named Jackie caught my eye. She lived on the same street where the playground was located. I used to see her all the time because the neighborhood girls would come watch us fool around and sometimes the girls would want to play too. That was a chance to look at them even closer. Being mannish little boys back then, this was a big step into the world of promiscuity.

The girls thought they could beat us, and we didn't mind at all. We actually liked playing with them too. So we allowed them to play with us—basketball, kickball, or whatever game was in progress. We did this so that everybody would get to know each other. Nobody was a stranger. It was a real neighborhood. Life is much different now; neighbors don't really know each other as much as they used to. They can live right next door to someone and not even know their neighbor's names.

So when Jackie came around, my palms would get sweaty, my hands would itch, and my neck would get stiff because she was a nice looking young girl. Even though we were only about thirteen or fourteen years old, I just knew she was something special. Since she was very attractive, a lot of the seventeen- and eighteen-year-old boys liked her too, when they were playing basketball and saw her coming, they'd start talking their stuff trying to get her attention.

Honestly, I thought she was out of my league. That's how pretty she was. I just knew she would never think twice about being with a boy like me. She could be with anybody in the neighborhood, and in my mind, I was a nobody. At least, that's what I felt because we lived in two different worlds. I was even a little scared to talk to her. I didn't feel confident enough.

Jackie would switch down the street, smiling, popping her chewing gum in her mouth, twirling her hair in between her fingers, making the guys lose their minds. She knew what she was doing, and got a kick out of how much control she had over the fellas.

She had a cousin named Thomas who was a lot like me because we both liked school, and we were both smart and made good grades. He didn't really get involved with all the sports and everything, but I liked him a lot. He wore glasses and was kind of nerdy, but I was too. We had a lot in common. Thomas and I used to walk home together, and we became really good friends. I wanted to tell him so badly that I had the biggest crush on his cousin. She was my dream girl. Thomas was Jackie's first cousin so they were really close. I felt so good, because I knew that if she saw me with Thomas, she would know that I was a nice guy. Eventually, she started to walk home with us. I remember it like it was yesterday. The beginning of puppy love. That's how it all began for me and Jackie.

I felt like *the man* because I knew all the fellas couldn't believe she was walking with *me*. I would play with her and kid with her on the walk home. She used to get on me too. She knew how to carry her own. Jackie was pretty, but she was tough too. I think that made me want to be with her even more. We were both young, but when I look back on things, I knew she could be the one. My one.

In my eyes, Jackie and I were made for each other. On the walks home I started telling Thomas how pretty she was and since me and Thomas were friends, I knew he wouldn't get offended. He knew all the guys liked his cousin. But he knew I respected our friendship, and I was brought up to respect girls too. I would think to myself that I had a better chance being with her because if Thomas approved, I was in there. I was smart and respectful, and being friends with Thomas gave me the in that I needed.

The rest of the guys tried to get to her by running game, but I got to her by being friends with Thomas. We were already friends so it was on the up and up. See, that's where most guys make their mistake: they don't play it smart, they don't play it cool. When you're trying to get a pretty girl's attention, you have to do something different. Every boy and every man wants a pretty girl or lady, but if you do the same old thing you will not stand out. She trusted Thomas, and so she began to trust me. That's how I stood out.

I had known Jackie a long time. Even as a little girl, she was always so nice, neat, and dainty. She reminded me of those little girls on TV who always looked so perfect. When I would see her, my stomach would feel funny. I didn't know what it was, but now looking back, I know it was because I liked her. I really felt this girl would be mine.

Back in elementary school, she used to come to class dressed real sharp. Jackie was an only child and her mother cared about her daughter coming to school looking nice. There were some days she would come to school and knock me off my feet. Because I was a little mannish, I was always making my obnoxious comments; but to tell to the truth, I wasn't the only one looking at her.

When we got to high school, I really started paying attention to her because she started filling out a little bit more. Her dresses and outfits were showing her curves, and as a young boy, it's hard to miss things like that. Walking home together, we started having a lot of fun. Even though she had other boyfriends, and I had other girlfriends, I did something she would never let me live down.

One day she came up to the playground with this older guy and I was messing with her. Right in front of the guy she was with, I kind of grabbed her! She didn't appreciate that and got very upset with me. She came after me but I was running pretty fast and she couldn't catch me. She just stood in the middle of the playground and cried because she was so mad. Later I felt bad about it, but I didn't want her with those other guys. That was my way of saying she belonged to me. I wasn't trying to disrespect her; I just couldn't stand seeing her with those other fellas. She finally forgave me, because later on we started going to parties and hanging out more.

The parties we went to were held in the basements of different houses in the neighborhood. When we arrived, the lights would be off so we would be in the mood for hooking up. One night Jackie and I were down at the party, and I asked her to dance. She agreed and one thing led to another. I talked my good stuff and finally kissed her. And she kissed me back! I was beyond excited and that led to our relationship developing. Next thing you know, she became my girlfriend. We were fourteen.

I started walking over to her home to visit. Her mother never really liked me. She thought I wasn't good enough for her daughter because I was poor.

 At that time, there was a fish market directly next door to our house, and in the back they had a garage where they used to store all of their fish heads and guts. A lot of rats and rodents used to love to go back into the garage, which is how our house got infested with them.

Jackie's mother knew that we lived behind that old fish market, while they lived in a beautiful home on 146th where all the nice houses were. Her mother still lives there to this day. She knew that I didn't have a house like that, and wanted her daughter to have better than what I had to give her. Even though I was still young, her mother didn't want to give me a chance. She wanted her daughter to have a young man who could take care of her, and provide the lifestyle she was used to or better. But I wanted to be with her, no matter what her mother thought.

She knew there were other boys who were interested in Jackie, and she thought they were better for her daughter. She would say, "You don't need to be talking to Charles. He don't have no job, he don't have this, he don't have that."

But no matter what, Jackie still liked me regardless of where I lived or what I had. Knowing her mother didn't like me didn't stop her from taking a chance with me. She liked me as a person, and that made me feel confident as a man. I don't think she understood how much that helped my esteem. I was blessed to find someone like her so early in my life.

Jackie's mother was determined to keep her daughter away from me or any boy she thought was no good. I know it had to be hard trying to raise a pretty, and smart daughter without a father around and trying to keep her safe, and raise her to be somebody productive. I'm sure that's why after we graduated together from junior high, Jackie's mother sent her to an all-girls high school so we wouldn't go to the same high school that I attended.

Jackie was so upset that she was leaving me. She wanted to go to the same high school that I went to. But her mother meant business, so Jackie went to the Jane Adams School for Girls. We both hated it, because that's what separated us.

I know so many of you are trying to do the best that you can by raising your children the best way you know how. You may think you're being too hard, or you may think you're not being hard enough, but I will tell you that when you understand that God has a plan for your children's lives, and you're to protect that child with everything you have, you will not worry about what other people think. That's all her mother was trying to do; she wanted to protect Jackie's potential, her future.

After a while, I started to believe what Jackie's mother thought of me. So I began to mess around. Girls were showing me attention, and I must admit I liked it. What boy would not want attention from all the girls? Of course this didn't sit well with Jackie. But while she had no boys at her school, I knew boys used to come around after school and pick the girls up and drive them around in their cars. So she hung out with the boys after school, and I started hanging with the girls and that's how it went with us for a while. But then, after playing around with other girls, and after she gave other boys attention, we started going together again and became girlfriend and boyfriend.

When her mother started seeing us getting closer, she didn't like that at all. Jackie's mother was a barber and owned her own shop in town, which meant that Jackie was at home a lot by herself. And being an only child, it was easy for her to sneak me over, because no one was there to stop us. But all mothers have a sixth sense. And Jackie's mom had to do something to get her daughter away from me.

Sometimes we as young males don't have a man around to teach us the right way to handle what's going on in our bodies and how to channel our thoughts in a positive manner. When you're a young boy, you need a man who can teach you and show you how to treat a girl. How to respect her and take your time with her. But I got my education about girls from around the way. So I didn't learn those things until later in life.

A PIVOTAL MOMENT IN MY YOUNG LIFE

When Jackie got pregnant it was a shock to both of us, and we didn't know what to do. We had no money, no diploma—we were still children. We had to let her mother know, and she didn't want Jackie to end up in a bad way like some of the other girls in the neighborhood, so she decided it was best that she didn't have the baby. This hurt me and my girl to no end. But what could we do? We were so young. So we had to get rid of the first child we ever had because her mother was upset that she had gotten pregnant at such a young age and she wanted Jackie to finish school.

Her mother wanted her to be something more in life than just taking care of babies. That was hard on us being so young, and we went through that until we graduated. A young male doesn't always understand what young girls go through when they have to give up a baby because they are too young to raise a child. It was like a piece of her left and just never came back. To stop the pain, we both became numb. But eventually we had to be strong, and I had to be there for Jackie. I loved her, and I wanted the best for her. And she cared for me no matter what anybody thought of me. She never made me feel less than her because we had different lifestyles. She accepted me. She meant the world to me.

When you're down in a bad way, you need someone to believe in you. You need someone to tell you it's going to be alright. If you have ever felt hurt, pain, and agony in your life, learn to appreciate that person close to you. You may not understand it right now, but God will use all of your hurts and pains along with your triumphs and victories for your good. Just trust and know that it will all work out. That's what Jackie was for me. She was my friend, not just someone I was attracted to. I believe God used her to show me His unconditional love that He had for me.

"If you have ever felt hurt, pain, and agony in your life, learn to appreciate that person close to you."

I never disrespected Jackie or her mother, but one day when I was 18, I was at their house and Jackie got into an argument with her mom. It escalated quickly and became physical. I remember Jackie's mother screaming at the top of her lungs, *"You're going to talk to me like this in front of this little boy?"*

She called both me and Jackie every vulgar name you could think of. I couldn't believe it. This beautiful woman in this beautiful home was acting like some crazy woman out in the alley. I would not have believed it if I hadn't witnessed it with my own eyes. I hated what was happening because I could see the hurt in my girl's eyes. And I couldn't understand why she would act this way towards me. Whenever I came over and her mother needed something done or fixed—any "man" chore—I would always happily do it for her.

Jackie yelled at her mother, "Charles ain't never done nothing but whatever you ask him to do and you're going to talk to him like that and call him names?"

They began to fight right there in the kitchen in front of me. I mean a knockdown fistfight! I was trying to pull Jackie off because I knew it wasn't right for her to be fighting her mother but she just lost it.

Her mother was screaming, *"You're going to hit me in front of this lil black motha$@#*?"*

That day changed things between me, Jackie, and her mother. I didn't say anything about it then because I didn't want to make matters worse, but Jackie and her mother's relationship was never the same. That was the day Jackie left her mother's house.

Although her mother felt that way about me then, she now thinks I am the best thing that has happened to Jackie. She calls me son and highly loves and respects me. We have evolved over the years. Look at how God works.

Sometimes when you're too close to a situation, you can't see the forest for the trees. Things get out of control and events can happen in a split second that can change your life. Sometimes you do things to those you love that you can't take back. Take it from me, I know a thing or two about doing things without thinking them through. But God has been faithful to me, and He has been a restorer of my faith. Use my life and the words on these pages to allow God to show you that He can restore you too.

After the blowout between Jackie and her mother, she moved in with her grandmother. The family had a three-story house. Jackie's mother and uncle lived on the second level of the house. Her aunt and the aunt's daughter lived on the third level. Jackie's grandmother lived on the first floor, so after the fight with her mother, she moved downstairs with her grandmother and never went back upstairs to live with her mother again.

Once she was living on the first floor with her grandmother, I could come over a little more often. When Jackie was living with her mom she wouldn't let us run around, but her grandmother and grandfather would sometimes retire early for the evening, and I'd come over. We'd sit in the living room trying to be quiet and would talk all night.

Jackie would always ask me, "Are you hungry? My grandmother cooked some good stuff today."

That's what always stuck with me. No matter how my life was, I knew as long as I was with Jackie, she made me feel safe. She made me feel on top of the world, and that's why I loved her. I'd never felt like that before. The closest feeling to love like that was from my mother, and she was supposed to love me no matter what. But this was different; this was from a girl I could see myself spending my life with. She made me feel special.

I still remember how she used to jump up to get my plate ready, and make sure the food was nice and hot. She would bring it back into the living room, and we would sit on the floor and I would eat as she watched me eat. We'd talk all through the night about everything we could think of. I was a big dreamer, and she loved listening to all my ideas. And I had lots of them.

Then of course, back to reality. I'd go home about two o'clock in the morning and on the way I'd replay our conversations in my head. Every night I visited, I would sit there with her, and tell her the things that I was going to do with her in life.

One day I told her, "You're going to be my wife."

She just looked at me and smiled. She knew that I loved her, but she didn't believe that I was serious. I would tell her these things over and over, "You're going to be my wife and I'm going to take you around the world."

I told her all the places that we would visit together like Hawaii.

TAKING ON RESPONSIBILITY

I had been saving a little money so I could buy her an engagement ring. I knew I was going to marry this girl. I would think *she takes care of me, she feeds and looks out for me, and she's got my best interest.* When you feel the way I felt, you just know it's right.

I didn't have much money, but I made sure I had enough to buy something really special for the girl I wanted to spend my life with. So when I finally had enough money I went downtown on Christmas Eve and bought her an engagement ring.

On that Christmas Eve night 1971, while we were sitting in the living room, I looked her in her beautiful eyes and said, "Baby, would you marry me?"

She didn't take me seriously. "Stop, go on boy."

I reached into my pocket and gave her the box. "No, I'm serious, will you marry me?"

She opened the box and screamed. She put it on her finger and she jumped up off that floor like cops were knocking at the door. My baby ran down the hall yelling to her grandmother, "Charlie asked me to marry him!"

I was so excited just watching her run back and forth. Those were some good ol' days, when everything was fresh and new. We were still young, and some would say we were still wet behind the ears. But once I asked her to marry me and she took the ring, I knew right then I had to be the man, and a husband, and she was my responsibility from now on.

We got married on August 5, 1972 at nineteen years of age.

FIRST THINGS FIRST

My wife and I moved into several different apartments and houses within a period of one year. The reason we moved so often was because we were involved in selling drugs. Our houses were used as dope houses and we couldn't stay in one place for too long or people would catch on to what we were doing.

Even though I was married, I had other women working for me as prostitutes. They were buying me cars, jewelry, clothes and drugs to take and sell. This entire lifestyle of pimping was keeping me in the streets away from home and my wife.

One of the ladies was considered as being my "main lady". I had been with her for some time, even in my high school days. Six months after Jackie was pregnant with my oldest daughter Tiffany, this lady became pregnant with my son Chuck.

While we were living on the Eastside of Cleveland in one of our dope houses, our oldest daughter Tiffany was born, and this is where my wife learned that I had become addicted to drugs. Jackie walked in on me in the bedroom and caught me sitting on the floor with a needle of heroin in my vein.

Later on that year, we were unable to afford to move into another house so we moved back to my Mom's. Then my mother moved out. We converted the house into a dope house. By this time my son Chuck was born. We did not start with the best relationship, but as time went on, we connected closely as father and son.

While living in this dope house, one day our cousin came over to witness to us about Jesus. She was very bold. She ended up witnessing to Jackie and later influencing Jackie to become a Believer of Christ.

A short time after this Jackie asked me to go out to dinner with her and some friends. She did not tell me the whole truth on where we were going. It was a Christian restaurant that had church services after dinner. I was unaware of where I was. I began to see Bibles popping up on tables all over the place. I turned to tell Jackie, "What is going on?" She assured me everything was going to be alright. The preacher started preaching and made an alter call. The last person to answer the alter call was—guess who—Me. This was my first experience of accepting Jesus as my Savior.

BECOMING VICTORIOUS

You know, when I think about all the things that lead up to that moment, and everything after that moment, I see where all the pieces of the puzzle fit. You may have felt like you were too young in your life when you got married or had a child or tried anything in your life. You may have felt like had you done things differently your outcome would have been better. Well let me explain something to you. Your life is like a book. You have a beginning, a middle, and an end. Don't mistake your middle for your ending. You see, if I had stopped in the middle, I would have never allowed God to bring about my expected end.

You may be struggling right now with where you are because people have told you, *you're* too young, or you don't know what you're doing, but sometimes you have to experience these things for yourself. Just know that when you make your decisions and accept certain choices, it does not have to be the end. It may be hard, tough, and even painful, but if you just keep going you will come out victorious.

> "Don't mistake your middle for your ending."

3

EDUCATED IN THE STREETS

I know with me kicking it in the streets and dealing with other women, some people thought I didn't love my wife, but that's not it at all. I was immature back then; I was living for self. I didn't know who I was and my role as a spiritual being yet. Regardless of what I was doing to her, she always stayed with me; she never divorced me. She might have messed around while I was gone at times, but she was only human.

You know, a woman can only take so much from a man. I wasn't there to give her that emotional support, that physical love, and protection.

I had some friends who were like brothers to me, and sometimes they would come over to the house asking for me when they knew I wasn't home. But they knew the old lady was at home by herself because I was somewhere else with another chick. That's why you must always understand that what goes around comes back around.

One particular friend I had would stop by my home to tell on me about what I was doing. He was setting my old lady up the whole time. He didn't care; he just wanted to be with her. So when she started crying he'd be there to comfort her. He'd be her shoulder to cry on. That's what we dudes do when we want to get close to a woman.

He made her feel comfortable. She felt safe with him; because she knew he was a friend of mine. But he used our friendship to get close to my wife, and I wasn't paying attention because I was doing my own dirt, and my mind was on other things and situations. He was real slick too. He got me, he got me good. So my wife hit me with it during pillow talk, then she finally confessed to me what she was doing.

You know that song that goes: *Who makes love to your old lady, while you were out making love?* It hit the nail on the head!

It was happening right under my nose and I didn't realize it. Every time I came home to take a shower, change my clothes, and kick it with her for a day or two, she normally wouldn't want me to leave.

When after a while I'd say, "I gotta go," she'd ask, "When will I see you again?"

But then, her tone changed and she'd be like, "Okay, Charlie."

She would let me go. She stopped asking me to stay home. It was like she didn't even care anymore. When things change for a woman, it's the subtle things. Men don't always pay attention to those small changes, but that's where it all starts. We had a friend of the family who had a house in Garfield Heights (a suburb in Cleveland, Ohio), and he rented the house out to us. My Uncle Fred and his wife Lisa lived upstairs and we lived on the first floor. It was at that point when I really emulated my uncle because we were constantly in each other's presence. We became running buddies. I wasn't doing the right things by my wife. I was seeing the girl that I used to hang out with, still doing anything that I wanted to do, and not thinking about anyone but myself. I was following the path of destruction but thought as long as I was coming home and taking care of the bills, I could do what I wanted. After all, that's what other men around my neighborhood did. So the two ladies of the house, Lisa and Jackie, became very good friends.

Now Lisa knew what Uncle Fred was; he was a pimp. But she had been with him for years and she was one of those ladies who accepted reality. She was his wife because she understood him and believed there is no use in trying to talk him out of who he is.

She would say, "He's been doing it too long; there's no changing him."

So Aunt Lisa shared her story with Jackie, and let her know that I would pick up that same kind of spirit hanging with Fred. "He's probably doing the same thing," she announced.

And guess what? I really was. You see, Fred was teaching me the streets, teaching me the psychology of the hustle and the pimp game and even introduced me to doing drugs. I would cruise down the streets to see how he and other pimps would put women out on the block, check on them, give them instructions, and collect their money. I would eavesdrop to see what was going on. I started learning and absorbing all of this, listening to how they were talking to them, and thinking: *That is the life.*

I was like a sponge, soaking up everything I saw and heard. And soon, it was time for me to see if I was ready to put what I learned to the test. So I went out and met a couple of girls who were feeling my vibe and swag enough to be their pimp. I told them what my expectations were and they were cool with it. My main girlfriend was cool with it also. She had no problem with how I was living at all. In total, I had about four prostitutes at the time.

I told the girls I was going to my mom's house. I walked into the house with my little dapper dons on looking cool and my mom was in the kitchen cooking. I looked into the living room and saw Sonia, who we called Sara.

I called out to her, "Hey, baby."

Then I heard another lady named Michelle respond flirtatiously, "Hey Big Daddy."

I was surprised because I couldn't see her from where I was standing. Then I walked into the living room and saw Jackie was there too, sitting with Sara and Michelle. I was like a deer caught in the headlights and turn around and walked back into the kitchen.

My mother said, "What are you gone do about that situation in there?"

I told her, "I'm going out the back door."

"Oh no you ain't," my mother announced. "You're going in there and handle that situation."

I felt stuck between my mother, my wife, and the other chicks. I had no choice but to man up and just deal with it. I couldn't hide it anymore from Jackie so I put it all on the table. Once we sat down and really talked about what was going on, the other chick left so it was just me and Jackie left talking. She was so upset and crying and I felt bad about the whole thing and my part in it. I should have never involved her in anything like this. I had been around my uncle too long. I knew my wife wasn't like Aunt Lisa. She didn't come up like that, and she wasn't raised to accept a pimp and chicks on the side. I was trying to bring her into a lifestyle that wasn't meant for her. I was trying to get her to accept what I was doing, but it backfired even though I kept the ball rolling.

With all that I took her through, if this woman stayed with me as my wife, and my first daughter Tiffany I knew, deep down inside, it was time for a brother to come to his senses.

IT JUST GOT REAL

I hate that it took something go drastic for me to get caught for me to come to my senses. I hated that it had to happen the way that it did.

I can still see it so vividly. We were moving to the projects because we couldn't afford our apartment. So the first night my uncle and I were loading up everything. Since me and him were always kicking it in the streets, he had offered to help me move.

Jackie hated him, and it was for a good reason. He was teaching me the ways and hustles of the streets. So she didn't trust him. Even though helping us move was a good thing, she felt he was the reason I was in the streets in the first place. My sister also helped us move so all four of us were moving and loading up our things to move to the projects.

When we dropped off the first load with some of our furniture to the apartment, my uncle and I decided to take the next load. My wife and sister were hungry so they said they were going to walk across the street to the corner store and get something to eat. They were looking pretty foxy and since it was cold outside had on rabbit coats, looking as if they had some money.

Two men were checking them out as they walked into the store, and coming out they were held up at gunpoint and were put into a car with these two guys who demanded money from my sister and my wife. They had a little bit of money but my sister is smart and thought quickly.

She said, "I have an aunt that lives in this neighborhood. If you take me by my aunt's house, she has money."

They agreed and proceeded to take my sister over to my aunt's house. My sister went up the stairs to get the money, but my wife was forced to stay in the car with those two guys. While my sister was upstairs, she told my aunt what was going on, and that her and Jackie had been kidnapped and were being robbed. My aunt wouldn't dare let her get back into the car.

The men must have realized that my sister wasn't going to come back so they sped off thinking she was going to call the police. They left with my wife Jackie—my baby, my queen—and took her to a condemned building, made her pull out an old, dirty mattress, and then they raped my wife multiple times.

When my uncle and I came back with the last load, we didn't see my sister or Jackie. We had no clue what was going on. We didn't know where they were. We looked everywhere for them in the neighborhood. We finally went to my aunt's house, and my sister was there. She told us what was going on and that Jackie had been kidnapped by two guys.

Oh, man we were looking all over the neighborhood for her. We were crazy. My heart was racing. We had guns and everything; we were going to kill those fellas. I mean, they were dead if we found them. We called the police too. They were looking for her and couldn't find her either.

The guy who raped my wife that night had the audacity to walk her back where they picked her up from. He dropped her off and took off running.

My wife was violated in the worse way, and I wasn't there to protect her. I knew that I could not move her to those projects. I could not bring the most precious thing to that hellhole. That night that I told my uncle, "I can't do this no more. I am going to the military."

That was a difficult time in my life, in my marriage, and for my wife. You just don't have things like that happen and get over them easily. I left everything because it hurt me so deeply that my wife had to go through that. I was at the hospital with her that night when they were doing all the test and checkups, and I couldn't take it anymore.

My life was spiraling out of control, and I just said no more. *I can't live like this anymore.* My wife didn't deserve to live like that anymore. She was too good of a girl for me to let that kind of thing happen to her. My wife never did anything to anybody. I never felt pain like that before, except when we had to get rid of our very first baby.

I knew I had to make a change, and it had to be that very same night. It was now or never. Things were moving in slow motion. My mind was all over the place. I was still trying to process everything and make sure my wife was okay and still think about where we were going to live, because I wasn't going to take her back to those projects.

We also still had to tell her mother, who already didn't think I was good enough for her daughter. I needed strength for me. I needed strength for my wife. And it couldn't come from anywhere but God. I needed God to help me.

When my mother-in-law found out what happened to her daughter she was furious with me. She screamed, "How did this happen to my baby?"

With tears running down her face and gasping for breath, she cried like a baby. I hurt for her. That was the first time I saw just how much she loved Jackie. I saw her ache for her daughter. I saw her take on the hurt of my wife, and it was excruciating. She was grieving for her daughter being violated, and worse of all I had the added guilt for not being there to protect her.

But she surprised me. After we explained that I wasn't there because we were trying to move in, she realized it wasn't my fault for being gone. But nothing can take away what happened that night. Not time, not anything but God.

I now know that God will never give us anything that we cannot handle. I didn't know back then because I was a young man just trying to make it, not understanding the ways of God. But God used all these things that I thought would kill us to make me and my wife stronger. I know that you may have experienced some things in your life that caused you to doubt His plan for your life. But I have come to know that God is wise in all things, and out of your hurt and pain He will bring healing to you and someone else. God is no respecter of persons, and in Deuteronomy 31:6 KJV, He promised us that He will never leave or forsake us, and

God is true to His word. I wouldn't be here today, sharing my message with you if I didn't believe that He could do the same for you.

4

THE MILITARY

Shortly after the fiasco of my wife being kidnapped and raped, I decided I needed a change—and a big one. I was ready to enlist in the military.

Sometimes you cannot see the whole picture, that plan that God has for your life. I knew God played a part in my life with me going to the military. When I enlisted in 1975 at 22, I had been shooting heroin in my veins for seven years while in the streets. I wasn't even sure that the Army would accept me. But they did.

Shortly after pledging my oath, I received an order to report for eight weeks of basic training at Fort Jackson, South Carolina.

I arrived by bus and we drove up to these old barracks sitting on stilts. All fifty men who were on the bus were thinking: *What is this? Look at this place!*

We were met by drill instructors dressed with Smokey the Bear hats on their heads looking like they all had been sucking lemons. We knew right then we were in trouble. The drill instructors made us get on and off the bus with our duffel bags at least ten times—which wore us all out—then we were told to stand at attention.

The instructors introduced themselves and announced they were our mother, or father, our sister, or brother, any other relative we had…and by the way they also our God. So we knew they were crazy, completely out of their minds.

We lived in those barracks for the eight weeks but it seemed like forever. We had to learn discipline, how to make up our beds properly with the corners tucked in tight. Our footlocker had to look like a masterpiece: socks and T-shirts rolled up properly; hair combs, toothbrushes, and toothpaste placed in their respective spots, belts placed neatly. Nothing could be out of place during inspection. If it was, the instructor turned over the footlocker and you had to repeat the process.

They woke us up at 4:00 a.m. for physical training (PT) by throwing a large, aluminum garbage can. I hated running the most. But the run was also a good thing for me. It alerted my drill sergeant that I was a junkie on drugs. My drill sergeant asked me why I could not run half a mile without regurgitating. I shared my drug addiction with him and he allowed me to stay in the barracks until I withdrew. He never knew how God used him for me.

I WAS BEING DELIVERED

God was in the process of my deliverance when I didn't even realize it. I want to take this time to say to God be the Glory for the things He has done for me. *To him be glory and dominion for ever and ever. Amen.* (I Pet. 5:11 KJV) He was there all the time, even in the run.

Sometimes the other recruits didn't understand how I could remain in the barracks while they had to do physical training. They could not understand that God had given me favor with my drill sergeant.

After basic training, my first duty station, or post, was Honolulu, Hawaii. I was assigned to a unit called 3/4 Calvary at Schofield Barracks located on the Island of Oahu. Hawaii is a beautiful place to have a duty station, and I really fell in love with it.

Back then, I was still learning, and I was still trying to kick some old habits. When I was stationed in Hawaii, I had easy access to marijuana. It was easier to get on the military base than in civilian life. Since I was still smoking in the military my life was constantly changing, but that was one habit I couldn't kick.

I decided to get an apartment with a friend of mine named Rob, so we could share the bills. It was an easy decision to move off post with the fellas. Every man knows that one day he will have to change his ways. It's just a matter of when. So I saved up my money and after six months sent for Jackie and our older daughter Tiffany, and our new baby girl Charita. Hawaii was expensive if you lived off base, but that is what we had to do. I saved my checks to make sure I had more than enough to bring them to Hawaii so that we could live comfortably.

When my family finally arrived, I was both excited and nervous. I really didn't know what life would bring. I looked at my two baby girls and my heart just jumped, because they were the things that brought me joy.

I hated not being there for the birth of my second baby girl, but my daughter Charita is as close to my heart as her sister Tiffany. I know that God sent me girls because that would help me change how I viewed women. Even when I was living wrong, they were always in the back of my mind. I thought about them constantly and knew I could not mess up.

At first, Jackie had a hard time adapting to Hawaii, like the huge, flying cockroaches and baby lizards that lived in our house or apartment. But the lizards would eat all the bugs.

Across the street from where we lived was a sugar cane field and at harvest time they would set the field on fire. Spiders as big as or bigger than your hand fleeing the flames would invade the apartment building where we lived. I had many battles with them in our apartment. I told Jackie that if she could not handle Hawaii, she had to go back to the mainland, but she stayed.

As always, I loved looking into Jackie's lovely eyes, but I noticed something was different. I could not put my finger on it. After some time, she finally told me that she had given her life to God.

I thought, *My wife? To God?* She could curse out a sailor. She didn't play when it came to telling anyone that she meant business, yet she said, "Baby, I'm saved, and we need to find a church home."

At first, I thought, *Yeah…right!* My wife was always honest and a straight shooter so it wasn't that I didn't believe her. It was I didn't really *want* to believe her. I wasn't so sure I wanted a life in the church. I was in my military career being a man, and still doing what men do.

Honestly, even though my family was with me, I was still doing things I should not have been doing: smoking marijuana and hanging with the fellas. I wasn't too sure how us going to church was going to play out. But the more time went on, the more I saw how serious she was. Jackie was so motivated by the idea of it but I wasn't too hip on this whole salvation and religious stuff yet at that point in my life. I tried to provoke her to her old ways, but she would not use profanity anymore; she had really changed.

One day, one of the fellas who lived across the hall from us and I were hanging out at our home while Jackie and some of the ladies from the church were having bible study. D was my getting high buddy, and when the ladies would come over, we'd head straight over to his house, which was set up for men only. We had chessboards and our marijuana set up, and we would just have a good time being *men.*

Chess is called a *thinking man's game,* and it takes a long time to play because you have to really put thought into each move. We played until we would hear the women through the vents saying: *Goodnight, God bless.*

Once I knew they were gone, I'd walk back across the hall to our apartment and ask, "Baby, how did everything go?"

"Fine baby, just fine," she'd respond.

Even though my eyes were bloodshot red—anybody with eyes could see that I was high as a kite—my wife still prayed for me. She covered me, when I wasn't even thinking about trying to be saved. I believe she helped me truly discover God. She didn't give up on me, just because of what she saw in front of her. I could only imagine what I looked like walking into her life as messed up as I was; I must have looked like the walking dead.

When you're using only your five senses, you're not allowing the real you to manifest. There was no way that I could keep smoking, and living that type of lifestyle if I was ever going to be who God created me to be. I'm sharing these past parts of my life so you can understand that when you're smoking, drinking, womanizing, gambling, and doing all the things to satisfy the flesh, you will never see your real potential come to life. You will just be a shell of yourself until you make a genuine decision to truly change.

But at that time, I was still drinking and smoking marijuana and moving slowly towards God. But my wife and children were born-again Christians. They had accepted Jesus Christ as their Lord and Savior.

My oldest daughter Tiffany would ask me, "Daddy, are you going to church?"

I was so involved with watching my Sunday sports I would tell her no.

She'd tell me, "We are just going to keep praying for you."

My wife knew that God's grace and mercy could save me, so she was steadfast, and she never let me go. As I look back at it now, she did something that was truly amazing. She decided to fast until I was saved and totally committed to God.

During her fast, I was over D's house and we were getting high. I told D that my wife was going to fast until I get saved. He said, "Well, how many days has she been fasting?"

"Man, two weeks."

"So you're going to let her die?"

I laughed so hard when he said that because he said it so seriously. But then, I thought about it and it began to really weigh on me, how much she really loved me. I thought, *I'm not taking this love from her very seriously.* D's comment caused me to contemplate trying this God that my wife kept speaking about. I didn't know Him, but I knew Jackie, and her love for me was real even though I had disappointed her time and time again. She never took her love away.

In Hawaii, you always saw women going shopping in bikinis—that's the way it was over there. I'd be driving and would almost hit the curb trying to look at them. Jackie would just tell me to keep my eyes on the road. She believed in me so much even after all the things I did to her. She had to know that I was in my growing season. She had to, and I am grateful for her.

God used her unconditional love so I'd find out who He was. So I went to church with my wife one Sunday, and the day I decided to go was on Women's Day, of all days.

That day changed my life forever.

They had a female evangelist presiding. Her sermon was titled *Don't Trouble the Woman* and she referred to Proverbs 31 NLT, about a virtuous woman who was more precious than a ruby. Listening to the sermon, it seemed as if this Evangelist was talking directly to me. I was listening intently because obviously this was something I needed to hear. She went on to say, *don't trouble the woman*, (Prov. 31:10-31 NLT) and at the moment, I looked at my wife over in the choir and thought of all the trouble I had brought to my woman. I instantly felt heaviness on my heart, guilt, and so much shame.

I came from a place where women were not valued as much as men. I didn't trust women. Honestly, no one taught me how or even suggested that it was important. I loved being around women and liked them a lot, but I didn't know anything about appreciating a woman. So when I heard that message, it became very clear to me. It was as if someone went and took out my old mind and put in a new one.

That is how God works. He said it's the "renewing of our minds" (Rom. 12:2 KJV). "My people are destroyed for lack of knowledge" (Hosea 4:6 KJV).

I finally heard wisdom on that day and I saw my wife differently. As far as I was concerned, Mr. Player, Mr. Come-off-the-Streets, pimping was all I really knew. I didn't truly understand the value of a woman and I was learning for the first time in my entire life how precious a woman was. I began seeing my wife and women in general from a very different perspective.

When she made an alter call and asked if there was anybody who needed Jesus to help them in their life, guess who came weeping and crying down the aisle? It was me making my way to give my life to God/Jesus Christ.

"Thy word is a lamp unto my feet, and a light unto my path.," (Ps. 119:105 KJV).

"I am the way, the truth and life" (John 14:6 NIV).

As I was walking, Jackie was in the choir and people around her were pointing and asking, "Is that your husband?"

Jackie couldn't believe who was walking down that aisle. I saw it in her face as I cried tears of a rebirth. When I reached for her, she took my hand and placed it on her shoulder. I stayed right there and let it all out. Everything left my body. The pain, the sadness, and the confusion of who I was. I had been renewed, restored, and felt this instant energy of favor. I had never felt like that before.

When I looked up, her shoulder was soaking wet from my tears. It felt like I was seeing the world with a new pair of eyes because everything was so bright, illuminated. What I was experiencing was very deep. I could feel the real me trying to come forward. My body was tingling, my thoughts were rushing, my palms were sweaty, but it was because I was so *alive*. I felt like there was a new fire inside of me; I felt like a brand new person. God was moving through me, and I could feel Him manifesting; I could feel the Holy Spirit.

That day I accepted the new me: the brand new Charles.

That was where my salvation started. I have experienced backsliding before, but never have I felt this type of experience. I knew that this was real. My natural senses were sharper. I could hear better, see better—and not just with the natural eyes and ears, but with spiritual eyes and ears. I could easily discern my new path in life. Never before could I see a clear path to who I truly was. Before that moment, I hadn't felt ready for full commitment because there was still other stuff I wanted to do and experience. But after living that experience, I knew it was real and that my life would be forever changed.

During the three years, we lived in Hawaii, by this time I had three daughters-Tiffany, Charita, and Ebony, and we were excited about our spiritual life with the Church of God and Christ. Even though they were stricter than some other churches, we learned a lot from our time there. My wife wasn't able to wear pants, makeup, and things like that. We later learned that it wasn't about the external when we got back to the mainland, but our foundation was set and solid in the Word.

5

THE TRANSITION

Reflecting back on the quote: *sometimes you can't see the forest for the trees…*God was orchestrating my life with journeys and people that looked like tall trees I could not climb. I didn't understand how the good and the bad were working together to draw me closer to God. Behind the trees was a forest.

For the first time in my life, I came to realize why I made the decisions I did. I hadn't understood He was taking me through a process. I was transitioning from pimpin' to preachin'. I was going from having a sense of God to having a life of God.

When living the sense of God, I wasn't aware of being influenced by my flesh. I was ignorant of how much control the

flesh could have over one's life. Galatians 5:16 taught me that I was living by the sinful desires of my human nature…the flesh. I didn't understand what walking in the spirit meant. All I was doing was fulfilling my fleshly desires.

Reflecting back, I saw how it began under the table rubbing legs and thighs. That led to my teenage years, being a young man with raging hormones. You don't know how to settle down, you feel like it's the time for exploration, venturing out into the world of women. My flesh was totally out of control.

Even after I was married, I still didn't settle down. I was on the road of destruction; my life was falling apart. The devil—through the dangerous streets of pimpin' and drug dealing and using drugs—was trying to destroy me. "The thief comes only to steal and kill and destroy; I have come that they may have life, and have it to the full." (John 10:10 KJV).

As I realized what was happening to me I knew I wanted and needed a change, which was why I enlisted, but I still didn't realize God was in the process. The military brought about a change to my life. I was truly convinced I needed Jesus Christ in my life. I committed my life over to him.

While in Hawaii, Jackie and I had a baby girl named Ebony born in 1977 at Tripler Army Medical Hospital. To this day, you cannot tell this girl she is not Hawaiian. After being stationed three years in Hawaii, it was time for my next duty station. I received orders to go to Fort Sheraton Recruiting Command in Chicago, Illinois.

"I was going from having a sense of God to having a life of God."

My assignment was to work as a clerk typist. But shortly after reporting to the recruiting command center, I met a captain who was the liaison officer for a three-star general. He saw how sharp I was in my uniform, how shiny my boots were, and he asked me where I worked.

He said, "Let's go see your commanding officer."

The captain told my CO (Commanding Officer) that the general needed a driver, and that he would like me to report for inspection. After meeting the general, I got the assignment as his driver. It was an honor to be in that position and it wasn't anything but the favor of God.

Being in the military taught me how to be a better man. It taught me how to be a more responsible man. I was extremely proud of myself, and my wife and children were proud of me as well. This is what men live for, it's what makes us feel like men.

After leaving boot camp in South Carolina, I was able to experience and see different things and different places around the world. Being stationed in Honolulu was extremely exciting because I was able to see a different side of life from where I grew up.

I remember the days when I used to visit Jackie before we got married, and how we'd sit on the living room floor, and I would tell her about all the traveling we were going to do. I was young and just dreaming out loud. But I knew that I was meant to see more and do more in my life. I didn't want to live and die only seeing Ohio.

This reminds me of another story of the first time I preached a sermon. After moving to Chicago we begin to look for a church to attend. We were recommended to a church in North Chicago named, St. James Temple COGIC (Church of God in Christ). After visiting the church, we were invited by the Pastor to talk with him. While in his office, we introduced ourselves and made him aware that I was in the Military and we were looking for a Pastor to put us under his Spiritual Covering. To my amazement, he looked at me and asked me a question. He said, "You are a preacher aren't you?"

Before I could answer him, my wife Jackie spoke out for me and said, "Yes he is."

At that time, I was not a preacher. After that, he invited me to come back to church that night to preach. My heart dropped and I felt paralyzed. I was terrified.

When I got home I tried to put something to say on index cards, numbered them from 1 to 10. I felt I needed these notes so that once I was introduced to speak; I could look on my index cards. When the time came to speak my perfectly numbered index cards fell to the floor. I stood there speechless. One of the preachers in the pulpit picked up my cards and handed them to me all out of order. I didn't know what to do. So, I gave my testimony of being an ex-heroin addict and how God had delivered me. That was my first time preaching and thirty-seven years later, I am still preaching

That is how powerful the spoken word is: when you say something over and over again, after enough times you're speaking life into what you say out loud whether you know it or not. You're breathing life into each word. I had no clue that what I was saying out loud would actually happen.

If you're reading my words right now, then you understand that God tells us in Proverbs 18:21 NIV very clearly that, "The tongue has the power of life and death." If I knew back then that what I spoke would really manifest in the physical realm, I would have been more careful with my words.

I was going to be in Chicago for three years and after talking it over with my wife and praying over my next move, I decided to go to Seminary College.

6

THE PREACHER

"Man is created from the soil, and soil, on the other hand, is never what it appears to be, because he sees soil as pure potential"
~ (Taken from the book Rabbi Freifeld Speaks)

That is how God works: he will have you study his Word so that you can't just be a believer but know Him personally. I wanted to know more about who He was, not just from what I've been told because I know and understand that He requires all of us to know Him for ourselves. I knew that God was calling me closer to Him; to be a man, to learn and preach the gospel. And for that I needed to go to school.

I was *so excited*. I could not wait to get started. Things were moving fast because I felt this was the path that God wanted me on. I got my GED and completed a year at Trinity Seminary College. But I didn't feel I was getting the true Holy Ghost experience I needed. I was only learning the Word, the history, and the geography—we studied Jerusalem and Israel—but I needed more. I needed one of those down South, fire-breathing, Holy Ghost-filled preachers pouring into me.

So after one year, I left college in search of a deeper experience. I wanted a closer, more intimate walk with Jesus Christ and the instructors were teaching the idea of Jesus being a great teacher, but it wasn't like He was the Son of God. We were never taught about the Spirit, they never mentioned the Holy Ghost. I knew that I could not preach this. I could not help people come to Christ teaching this way.

I wondered: *How am I gonna save souls this way?* I didn't want to preach this from a secular point of view. My desire was to show God's love. I knew that in order for me to change my lifestyle, I needed to apply the teachings that God gave me to the people who truly needed to hear it.

Leaving Seminary College was the greatest thing that I could have ever done, because the Holy Ghost became my teacher. I learned more about the Bible than they could ever teach me because the Holy Spirit poured the Word of God directly into my spirit.

The Bible says that Holy men of God speak as they were moved by the Holy Spirit. To know about God, you need to go directly to the source. That is what God asks us to do. He desires for His children to come to Him.

We have not because we ask not. (James 4:2,3 KJV).

We are supposed to come boldly, and that is exactly what I did. I stepped out on faith and decided to allow Him to guide me during my spiritual walk. I had complete faith that He would speak directly to me. The Holy Spirit wrote the Word of God, so it made sense for me to go to the source to get the understanding I needed.

TAKE IT DIRECTLY TO GOD

I know this is why so many of us suffer: we go to everyone else to get answers. But they are not the ones who can solve the

"He desires for His children to come to Him."

problem. Take it from me; when you're dealing with any hurt in your life, you must release that burden to God. I am not telling you what I have read. I know what He has done for me and the people in my life. He can change your situation too, because He knows what to do. He is the Creator of all things. He loves you and He understands who you are, because He made you in His own likeness. He gave His only Son so that you and I would be saved and have a second chance. I had to learn this for myself.

My desire is that you get that same message. I know that I can't stop life from happening, but I can definitely give you something to think about. Just look to Him, because He knows all and He sees all.

"No problem is too big or too small," the Word says. He cares about our cares. That's enough to make me dance right now. It's good to know that God loves us that much.

I learned through God's Word, that the Holy Spirit's a living spirit. He is not an *it*, and many preachers that have been preaching the gospel for thirty or forty years still say that to this day. He's the third person of the Godhead. You have to respect the trinity.

He is a being, a person, a living spirit. He is a person who wrote and inspired the Word of God. He used people to write it and it says, "…but holy men of God spoke, being moved by the Holy Spirit., (2 Peter 1:21 WEB), and as He was moving in them and using them, they were writing.

Therefore, it takes that same Spirit for me to understand what God is trying to say. That is why a lot of people that are not spirit filled, don't have the Holy Spirit, and are not living for God. They'll open up a Bible and then close it just as fast and say, "I don't know what it all means."

I have been around so many people that do that. The Bible says, "Get understanding" (Prov. 4:7 NIV). God says, "My people perish from lack of knowledge." So when you lack knowledge, you're unable to get understanding.

If we know that we need understanding, then why are so many of us lost? It's because we don't go to God's word. God gave us a manual on how to live the life He intended for us. It's just like how your car comes with a manual that specifically tells you everything you need to know about the car: the engine, the warranty, maintenance requirements, and even contact numbers when the car needs service.

God created this same concept. The Bible has everything you need for your life, but some don't even open it up. If you want instruction in your life, open up the Bible. You need to study it. That is why I became a student of the Word of God by studying the Word, and learning the principles by understanding the Word of God and applying the principles to my life. I found out they actually do work. They work greater than I could ever express, and they cover every part of your life.

I began to gain knowledge, but there was a much deeper knowledge, a wisdom that was underneath the words on the pages. I found this to be especially true when I started working with Jewish Rabbis and understanding that the Rabbis were the few that truly knew God and His Word as well as the deeper meanings. They actually walked with God on a daily basis. They knew the Old Testament, lived and studied Orthodox ways. And because of their obedience, God has done so many things in their lives. God delivered them and saved them. Even when God brought them out of Egypt, they still taught their children about their God, even to this day.

They showed me that it's important to remember what God had done for them, which is why they celebrate so many different festivals and holidays. They are God's chosen people. The Bible says that they are the "apple of HIS eye," (Zechariah 2:8 WEB) and some are jealous of the Jews because of that. He didn't choose Blacks, Whites, or Hispanics, but because of His grace and mercy, we are still covered by the blood of Jesus Christ. That is only if we accept His Son as the living Savior.

This is why the Orthodox Jews understand the Word of God. They always keep Him as the head of their daily walk, as part of their way of life, and everyone in the community follows suit.

I spent most of my time with the Rabbis who broke the Word of God down to me, and they would say, "Pastor Sims, what do you think that scripture means?"

When I interpreted what I thought that scripture meant, they would look at me and say, "It doesn't mean that at all."

"Really? Get out of here," I'd say.

"That is what is wrong with your pulpit every Sunday," they explained. "The preachers stand over their congregation and tell them that this is what the Bible is saying. But little do they know they are not telling the whole truth because that is not what the Bible is saying at all."

That blew my mind; I could not believe preachers and ministers didn't really know what God was saying in His Word. As a result of learning from the Rabbis, the congregation brought me back as their speaker. Whatever I would speak to the church, the pastors would sit there looking at me and would say to themselves: *I went over that scripture a hundred times and I haven't heard that scripture broken down like that and it makes so much sense.*

When I went back to their office, they would say, "That was a powerful Word you preached this morning. Tell me more about this part." And after explaining and breaking the scripture down, they would say, "Man, I never heard that in my life."

The Rabbis are the few who truly know God. You have to spend a lot of time with God to know Him. It's like you have to spend time with a woman to know the woman. You find out her nature, what she likes, and what she does not like. You also learn what pleases her and what makes her go the extra mile. When you spend time with a woman, she shows you how to love her. Therefore, you will never know her until you spend time with her. The same goes for God; you will never be able to know God until you spend time with Him.

The more time that I spent with God, I learned that obedience and sacrifice are valuable to Him. I don't want any of you simply going through the motions thinking that just going to church on Wednesday and Sunday is enough.

What does your daily walk with Him consist of?

Do you know His character?

Do you know His commandments?

Do you know what He wishes for all of his children?

God tells us that obedience is better than sacrifice (1Samuel 15:22). Are you obeying his word?

The Rabbis really allowed me to question if I really had a relationship with the living God, or I was just worshiping Him on a superficial level.

Are you ready to truly sacrifice?

You have to give up a lot when you follow God. You have to sacrifice some things in your life and give them up to show God who is more important to you; is it Him or the thing that you won't give up?

God is all about the sacrifice. That's why He sacrificed His only Son. Come on, who's going to do that? Are you willing to sacrifice your child?

7

‡‡‡‡‡‡‡‡‡‡‡‡‡‡‡‡‡‡‡‡‡‡‡‡‡

SACRIFICE

What if God told you to sacrifice your child like He did Abraham?

Then God said, "Take your son, your only son, whom you love—Isaac—and go to the region of Moriah. Sacrifice him there as a burnt offering on a mountain I will show you." (Gen. 22:2 NIV)

Abraham obeyed and just as he was ready to take the knife and kill him, an angel of the Lord showed up and told him not to harm the boy (Gen. 22:12). God never intended for Abraham to kill his son; He was testing Abraham. His obedience and faith in his Word showed God that Abraham could be trusted.

How many of us would do that today?

Most of us could never imagine picking any of our children to be a sacrifice no matter how much we believe. God wants to know what sacrifices we are willing to make. What are you willing to give up that means a lot to you?

If you hold on to whatever you're struggling with you're going to find that it's not worth it. If you're in an unhealthy relationship, why are you holding on to it? Don't you know that God wants you to give your all to Him so that you can be free to love and be loved by someone who will love you the way that He does? Trust me; whatever you're going through is not worth it: the hurt, the pain, the deceit—there is nothing good that can come out of that relationship, because God is not the head of it.

God says, "… where the Spirit of the Lord is, there is liberty.." (2 Corinthians 3:17 KJV)

Let those things go and watch what God does for your life. He does not want you to have a boring life. He desires you to have an abundant life, and He knows that through Him, and only Him, that fulfillment will come. When you sacrifice, God will reward you. Understand that you reap what you sow. So if you're sacrificing and being obedient to His Word, He will stay true to what He has promised for your life. But you must know His Word first and let it reside in you. We were never told holding on to something would bring more things, more love, more money, more anything.

"I thank God that I gave up my life for another life."

"Give and it shall be given." (Luke 6:38 KJV)

We absolutely have to make those sacrifices and that is what I am trying to explain here by sharing how much God has changed me. I thank God that I gave up my life for another life. This is why Jesus says, "'I am the truth and the life…If you hold on to your life, you shall lose it; but if you give up your life you shall find it." (Matthew 16:25 KJV)

Therefore, I had to give my life in order to find life.

Real life is hidden because at first, you don't realize it. We live a false life because everything on Earth is temporary. It's a foreshadow. We call it pleasurable, but the greatest job I have is being able to sway the way a man perceives life—that is a powerful statement.

I wait to bring understanding to those who have none. That is why I am writing this book: to persuade you to get on the right track and see yourself from the eyes of the one who created all living things past, present, and future. God knew that He had to give us something tangible, so He left us with His Word, and I am doing the same thing.

I pray that the words on these pages will serve as a guide to finding who you are. I pray your journey will not be in vain. All of your struggles, insecurities, doubts, and pains will not go unnoticed by God if you trust in Him. His will for your life will be greater than any hurt you have experienced.

I know the pains of life: the addictions, the wrong mindset, all of it. I know firsthand because I experienced it. But when you walk with Jesus and hold His hand, He will guide you through life's obstacles. He will never leave you or forget about you. That is why the Holy Spirit lives inside each and every one of us: to serve as a comforter.

GOD SPOKE TO ME BACK IN CHICAGO

Years ago, when I was still in the army, I was ministering to a church in Chicago, IL. Right before I was about to preach, I looked at the congregation, and God started showing me what people were thinking.

It was like I could visually see what people were thinking. God showed me a lot of minds over the congregation and told me that I have to persuade their minds.

Some people were thinking about getting out of church and going home, and some were looking at the time. I even saw one lady thinking: *I might have some food or something back home on the stove.* God was allowing me to see that people were not ready to hear the truth. They were not prepared to receive what I was about to say, because their minds were on things of this world.

We need to prepare our minds and hearts to receive the Word of God, so that His Word can work wonders in our lives.

When you prepare a meal, you have to add seasoning and cook it before it's ready to be eaten. God's Word is no different. We have to prepare our minds to digest the Word, so that we can get the spiritual nutrition we need to live in this world.

God says that, "Men cannot eat bread alone but must eat of the living word." (Matthew 4:4)

This is what we are living within our churches today. It's difficult to stand in front of people and deliver a message that God has instructed us to give when people's minds are not clear. He has to give us the ability to persuade people to listen, to open up their minds. I am most thankful that He has entrusted me with the gift of influence and persuasion.

HOPE!

I learned from this old guy who said, "Pastor Sims, when you stand up before a congregation, don't preach a shotgun message, use a .45 so you can hit what you're aiming at."

So whatever I am aiming at, I have to hit my target.

As I share this message with you, I want you to know that my target is *hope*. I am a man who has weathered all types of storms, metaphorically speaking. Even though I grew up as a young black boy without a father; was led into the streets and became a pimp; married the love of my life, but was unable to be the man she needed all the time, and became addicted to drugs, I never once was too far gone. I always had hope. Hope is very necessary as you go through the storms. Some storms will be small, others will feel like a tornado, but you will be equipped if you're armed with hope.

That is why I became a student of the Word. I was lead to my spiritual father through the Church of God and Christ that resonated with my spirit. I was an aspiring minister mentored by one of the church elders. He inspired me, and he saw something in me and nurtured my gift. He walked me along and decided that it was time for me to become an ordained elder. I was being courted by several churches during that time of learning and my wife's grandfather wanted me to become a member of his congregation, but Jackie and I were really enjoying where we were living. After leaving the military and leaving Chicago, we were back in Cleveland and wanting to support the family, we eventually made our way to his church where I became a member of United Holy Church of America.

I was happy that we decided to join his church after he died. The bishops that took over knew that Jackie was the granddaughter of the previous bishop, so they took me under their wing, believing I had potential to be a preacher.

They sent me to Massillon, Ohio, as the new pastor. Our new church home was only two hours away, and I was their pastor for seven years. During that time, I learned a lot about myself and other people. The role of a leader is often difficult because you're working with different personalities, and no one is perfect.

Looking back over those years, I saw that we were not progressing, but we learned a lot. I decided it was time to go independent and start my own church. We were out there by ourselves trying to grow a church and trusting that the people would do what they say they would.

We were just starting out, and it takes people, resources, money, time, commitment, and faith.

HUMBLING MOMENT BEFORE GOD

When we left the church where I was a pastor for seven years in Massillon, Ohio, I decided to work with a lady we had known for years named Apostle Winnie Hamilton. Early on, when we were in the Church of God in Christ, before we thought about becoming preachers, I had been watching her minister. She eventually left the Church of God in Christ and started her own ministry called Sonrise. She has been our spiritual covering for over 30 years. She is the one who consecrated me in Cleveland. I was ordained as a pastor under her one Sunday, and her church still holds our legal consecration as Apostles and Prophets.

Under her leadership, she and Jackie went back and forth to Africa. She wanted me to go, but I wouldn't go to Africa. The Bishop got upset because I would not go. To this day, she still goes all over Africa—South Africa, Libya, and Zimbabwe—to preach.

By the grace of God, I have been ordained as an Apostle. I am so humbled by this level in Christ. The scriptures tell us the order of responsibility in the church. It says, "…first apostles, second prophets, third teachers.." (I Corinthians 12:28 WEB) Those are all the ministries that God has given to the church.

This position of Apostle comes with a lot of responsibility and humility. It's a balancing act, and I take it seriously. It's an honor to hold such a position to God's people. So much more comes with being an Apostle because they go to churches and build them, by laying foundational truths in people's lives. A lot of Christians don't stay strong because they have no solid foundation of principles before they try to build a spiritual life.

"If you want to be pleasing to God, you must surround yourself with those who can assist you in seeing the truth."

Apostles are like pioneers and trailblazers. They go to places where no one has ever gone. They travel and they become spiritual fathers. Wherever they go, they are at the highest level of ministry. When an apostle walks into a room, there is such a high level of respect shown by the people of God. We as Apostles are commanded to hold the mantle of truth, integrity, and peace. We are assigned to the church to help build where it's needed, and I believe that is why God wanted me to share my life with you.

We all need someone to help guide us, to help give us direction, and teach us right from wrong. We need help along the way. How can you build better self-esteem, relationships, or even a better walk with God if there is no one who has gone before you? It's impossible. If you want to be pleasing to God, you must surround yourself with those who can assist you in seeing the truth. God's Word is the truth, and there's no other way to put it. Just like learning from the Rabbis, they said we didn't tell the truth. There is an order to everything, and with each step comes elevation.

This is not an opinion; this is in the Word. I don't just want to only give hope, but to also show you that you must read for yourself. In God's Word we are told specifically that we perish by our lack of knowledge. (Hosea 4.6) If you're anything like me, you don't take someone's word without reading and studying for yourself.

The next thing I look forward to doing is walking in my assignment by God. If God tells me to go to Africa this time, guess what? It's not up to me to say I don't want to go. I have to say: *Thy will be done.* I will go and that's the way it is. So whatever He tells me to do, I have to do. When you and I decide to live in that type of obedience, God's blessings for us will overflow. It's not always easy to just say: *Whatever you want, Lord,* but it's necessary. I still think about where I'd be if I had not given my life to Christ that day on Women's Day so long ago. I'd still be getting high, still womanizing, or worse, I might have ended up strung out on the streets, in prison, or even dead. I had to have blind faith and submit to His will.

God requires faith to move on your behalf. You can't think about it, you can't go with your feelings; you have to make a move to take up your cross and follow Him. It ain't always easy, but He will bring people to help you. He has His angels covering you every step of the way, but you must submit yourself. Don't wait. When my overseer—the one who consecrated us—sees something that God has instructed her to tell me, then I must do it. It's a lot of responsibility but you have to see the results of my life to understand why I'm willing to obey.

8

GOD CAN CLEAN YOU UP

In the Bible, there were three levels to the tabernacle: the outer court, the inner court, and the Holy of Holies. The high priest was the only one who could go into the Holy of Holies but he couldn't have any sin attached to him. He had to be pure or else he would be struck dead. (Exodus 28:35) When the people of God see me, I have to stand before them without living a sinful life. I have to represent. But I'm not just representing myself; I am a representative for the kingdom.

Listen, God is not asking us to be perfect, because there is no such thing. But He does require us to walk in excellence. Every day, the flesh causes us to struggle, to want to do things that make us feel good. I still struggle with my flesh, but that's where I use the Word of God to combat what my flesh desires because of the blood of Jesus who died on the cross, and shed His blood for our sins.

My hope and wish for you is to understand that no matter where you have been in your life, or what you have done, God can clean you up. He did it for me. Just present yourself to Him and confess. Confess it all, say it aloud, and just talk to Him. He's cool…I promise. Talk in your own words; He will meet you where you are.

> "Every day is a battle, but if you have the right weapons, you will come out on top."

I want you to know that our Father is concerned about you, and we all have the ability to be great in this life. We were made in His image. We have everything from Him: His character, His spirit, His love. If you just tap into it, you will never lose His love. No matter what has happened in your life, He can take you from nothing to something.

He will show you who you're really meant to be. The real you that lives underneath the surface. He knows everything you're dealing with, and He knows what you're facing.

I am a living witness of His miracle on my life. He took me, washed me, and made me clean. I am a work in progress, but let me tell you that God is still on His throne, and He is waiting for you to choose Him to come pick you up. He wants you to be free, to lay down your own life, and take on the one He has for you. Take off that old way of thinking, change your mind, and put in the mind of Christ.

I dare you to take this walk with me. I dare you to be bold enough to step away from the crowd and let Him use you. Make a decision today to accept that you need Him, and accept that He is the solution to your problem. I know that there is still a lot of emptiness. Even though you're making the money, have the job, and have the relationship, you still don't have the fulfillment. Everybody is chasing and looking for happiness.

God says, "But seek ye first the kingdom of God, and his righteousness; and all these things shall be added unto you." (Matt 6:33 KJV)

You don't have to walk around not being satisfied, but you cannot keep trying to satisfy yourself with things that don't matter. You cannot replace Him.

I just read a book not too long ago about these fourteenth, fifteenth, and sixteenth century reformers. One man named John Hust believed in speaking the truth, and he wanted to reform the church and people with truth. That is what we all want. That is what I wanted, even as a small boy—the simple truth about who I was. I wanted to know if I mattered to my Father? Did I matter to my family? Did I matter to God?

When you don't know the truth you end up living a life without purpose, without reason.

Well, Jesus says, "I am the way, the truth, and the life, and no man shall see the Father but through me." (John 14:6 WEB)

But instead, we are looking for people to tell us the truth. Politicians are not telling you the truth. You want to believe it—because they are telling you what you want to hear—and you vote for them. Once you vote for them and they get into office, they forget all about what they promised you. So you're not getting any truth out of them.

The Bible says, "It is better to take refuge in the LORD than to trust in humans" (Psalms 118:8 NIV)

I like the quote by Myles Munroe: "If you need to know something, go to what's created it. Why not go to the manufacturer?"

That is so true. You need to go to the manufacturer. If I have a Mercedes Benz and want to know about it, I'm not going to General Motors. I'm not going to Ford. You're the product of God. So if you want to know about yourself, go to the manufacturer of YOU; after all, He made you.

9

GOD'S PROMISE

This is a very special moment for me, because God promised me a long time ago that I would be able to help change people's lives, bring hope, and influence them to get back on the right track.

Well, I hope one of those people is you. I hope that you have found a little piece of your own story in between these pages.

I always knew that God was a keeper, because He kept me. He kept me alive to see another day. Now I know that my life wasn't just for me but for you too. Listen to me: if you're struggling in a bad situation right now, don't lose hope. Stand on God's Word, look deep inside of you, and cry out to the comforter that lives with you. Every day is a battle, but if you have the right weapons, you will come out on top.

Let the Holy Spirit whisper in your ear and guide you. Let God's word arm you and shield you, and allow Gods angels to come and cover you.

I don't have all the answers but I know who does. I pray that you find out who really is underneath all the wrongs, the hurts, pains, and bad decisions. I pray that the true you is unveiled, and that you become who you were predestined to be.

I wish you love, health, and most of all that God be the head of your life. I pray this for you right now in Jesus' name. Amen.

www.ingramcontent.com/pod-product-compliance
Lightning Source LLC
Chambersburg PA
CBHW050553160726
48003CB00002B/877